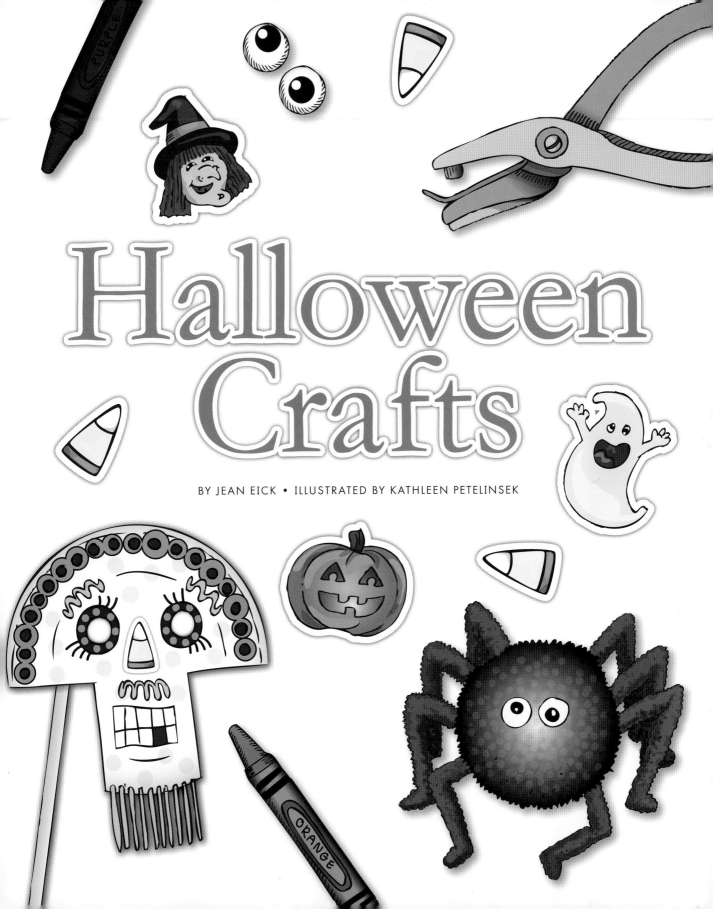

Halloween Crafts

BY JEAN EICK • ILLUSTRATED BY KATHLEEN PETELINSEK

Published by The Child's World®
1980 Lookout Drive
Mankato, MN 56003-1705
800-599-READ
www.childsworld.com

The Child's World®: Mary Berendes, Publishing Director
The Design Lab: Design and production

Library of Congress Cataloging-in-Publication Data
Eick, Jean, 1947–
   Halloween crafts / by Jean Eick; illustrated by Kathleen Petelinsek.
     p. cm.
   ISBN 978-1-60954-234-4 (library bound: alk. paper)
 1. Halloween decorations–Juvenile literature. 2. Handicraft–Juvenile
literature. I. Petelinsek, Kathleen, ill. II. Title.
   TT900.H32E332 2011
   745.594'1646–dc22   2010035493

Printed in the United States of America
Mankato, MN
December, 2010
PA02071

Table of Contents

Happy Halloween!

Halloween is a fun **holiday** for many people around the world. It is celebrated on October 31. On this day, some people dress up in **costumes**. Others have parties and tell spooky stories. Halloween is a fun time to celebrate autumn!

Halloween is a holiday that is a mixture of different things. In many **cultures**, people have long held celebrations to honor their dead. Some cultures also celebrate the end of summer and the beginning of autumn. Halloween is both of these! It's a time to enjoy the fall weather, remember loved ones, and sometimes to dress up as something silly—or scary.

Let's Begin!

1 This book is full of great ideas you can make to celebrate Halloween. There are ideas for decorations, gifts, and cards. There are activities at the end of this book, too!

2 Before you start making any craft, be sure to read the **directions**. Make sure you look at the pictures too—they will help you understand what to do. Go through the list of things you'll need and get everything together. When you're ready, find a good place to work. Now you can begin making your crafts!

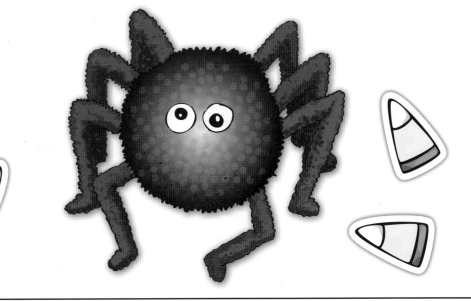

Spiders

These spiders are cute—and creepy, too! They make great
decorations for your house or classroom.

THINGS YOU'LL NEED

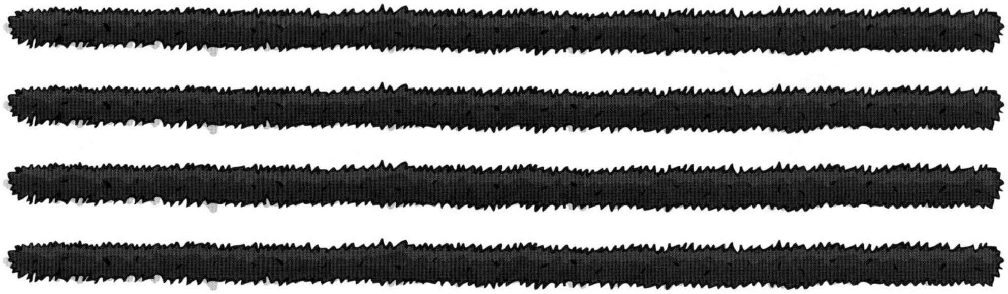

Four black pipe cleaners

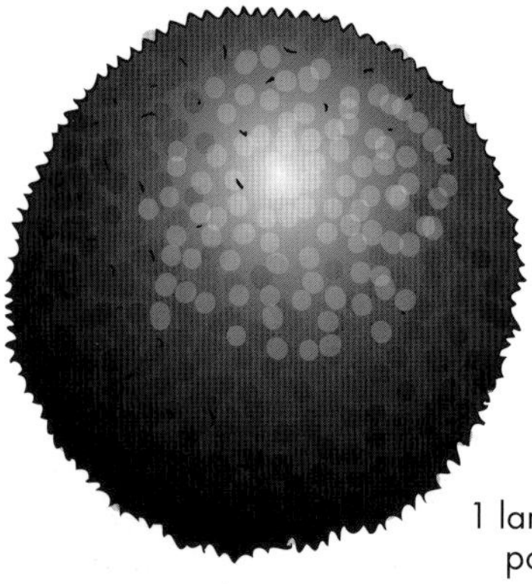

Two
moveable
eyes

GLUE

1 large black
pompon

Glue

DIRECTIONS

1 Take two pipe cleaners and wrap the middle of one around the middle of the other.

2 Do the same with the other two pipe cleaners.

3 Wrap the two sets of pipe cleaners together.

4 Bend the pipe cleaners down on the ends to form the spider's legs.

5 Glue the pompon onto the middle of the legs. Make sure you hold it there until the glue sticks!

GLUE

6 Glue the eyes on the front of the pompon. If you want, shape the spider's legs some more.

Pumpkin Cutouts

Paper pumpkins are easy to make. They are great for decorating.

THINGS YOU'LL NEED

Scissors

Pencil

Glue

3 sheets of construction paper
(one orange, one brown, and one black)

A large glass, cup, or bowl

DIRECTIONS

1 Take the glass, cup, or bowl and turn it over on the orange piece of construction paper. Trace around its edges with your pencil to create a circle.

2 Carefully cut out the circle.

3 Draw a stem on the brown piece of paper and carefully cut it out.

4 Draw some shapes for the eyes, nose, and mouth on the black piece of paper. Cut the shapes out.

5 Glue the stem on the back of the orange circle.

6 Glue the face shapes on the front of the orange circle to make your pumpkin's face.

Masks

These easy masks are great for plays and other special times, too!

THINGS YOU'LL NEED

Scissors

Glue

Yarn

Construction paper

A large white paper plate

Crayons or markers

Stickers

Pencil

Straw

DIRECTIONS

1 Take the paper plate and draw the shape of your mask with your pencil. Cut out the mask.

2 Hold the mask up to your face. Using the pencil, very lightly draw circles around your eyes. Cut out the eyes.

3 Decorate your mask however you'd like. You can use yarn for silly beards, hair, and eyebrows.

4 Construction paper, stickers, markers and crayons are great for making goofy mouths, noses, and other decorations.

5 Glue the straw to the back of the mask.

6 Wait for the glue to dry. Now your mask is ready! Use the straw as a handle to hold the mask in front of your face!

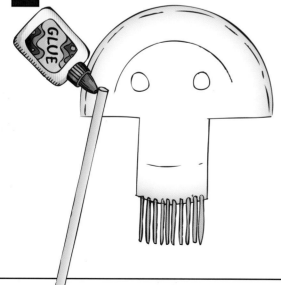
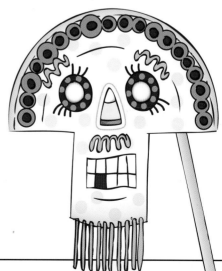

Painted Pumpkins

Instead of carving pumpkins, try painting some faces on them.
You can give them as gifts to parents and teachers.

THINGS YOU'LL NEED

Small pumpkin

Cup of water

Black
marker

Paintbrush

Acrylic paints

DIRECTIONS

1 Make sure your pumpkin is clean. Wipe off all dirt and dust.

2 Think about what you want to paint on your pumpkin. Draw the face on the pumpkin with the black marker.

3 Use the paintbrush and paints to paint along the lines you've just drawn. If you want to use one color on top of another, be sure the bottom color is dry before you start.

4 When you are finished painting, let the pumpkin dry all the way. Now it's ready to be given as a special Halloween gift!

Treat Bags

Make some of these bags as special Halloween gifts for your friends.

THINGS YOU'LL NEED

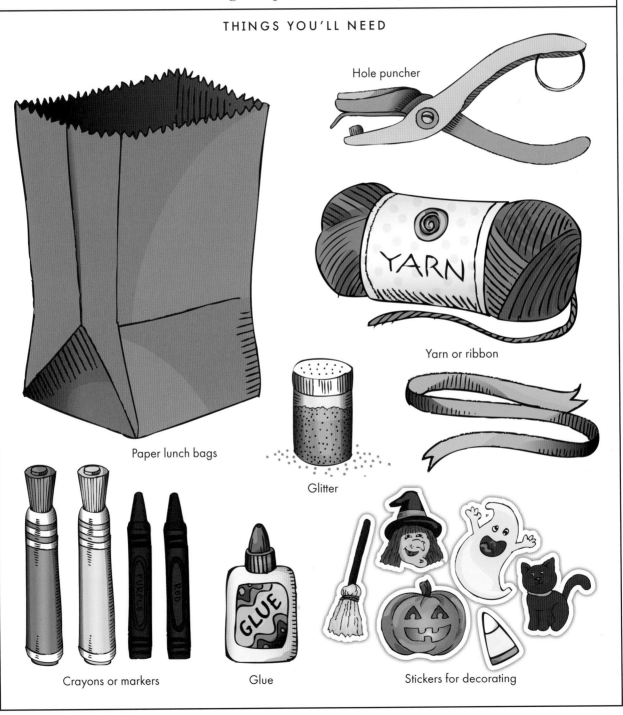

Hole puncher

Yarn or ribbon

Paper lunch bags

Glitter

Crayons or markers

Glue

Stickers for decorating

DIRECTIONS

1 Decorate the bag however you'd like. Glitter, crayons or markers, and stickers are all good ideas.

2 Fill the bag with candies, treats, or prizes.

3 Fold over the top of the bag. Punch two holes in the top of the bag. They should be a little bit apart.

4 Put some yarn or ribbon through the holes. Then tie the bag shut.

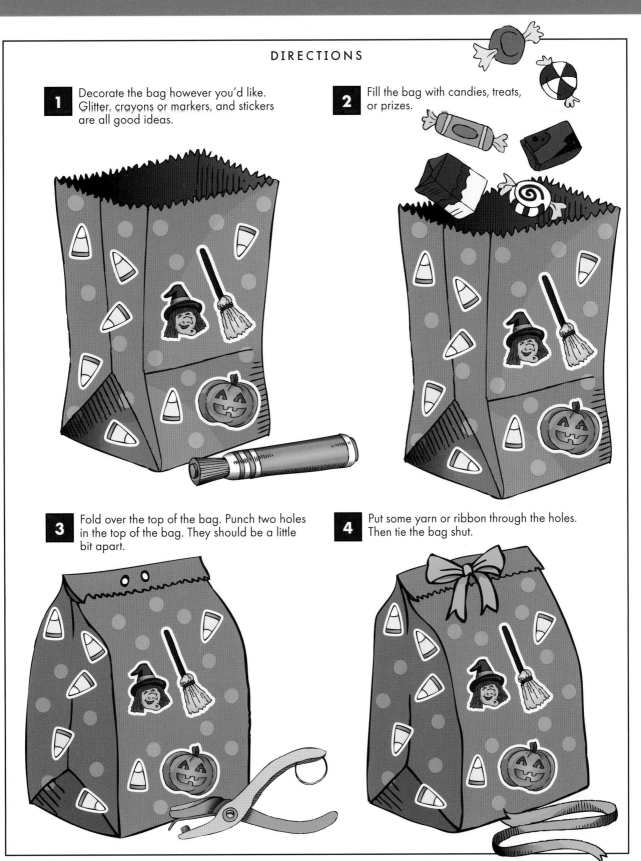

Halloween Cards

Cards are a great way to say "Happy Halloween" to your parents, grandparents, and friends.

THINGS YOU'LL NEED

Scissors

Construction paper (lots of different colors)

Glue

Glitter

Ribbon

Buttons

Pencil

Crayons, markers, or paint

Stickers or magazine pictures

DIRECTIONS FOR CARD ONE

1 Fold a piece of construction paper to the size you want it to be. Folding once will make a large card. Folding it twice will make a smaller card.

2 Decorate the front of the card any way you'd like. You can use ribbons, buttons, glitter, and stickers—be creative! Write a message on the inside of the card. You can decorate the inside, too. Don't forget to sign your name!

DIRECTIONS FOR OTHER CARDS

1 You can make Halloween cards in many different ways. Here are some ideas for making your cards even more special! For a spooky card, draw lots of cobwebs and bats.

2 For a ghost card, use black construction paper. Then use white crayons to draw silly ghosts.

3 For a picture card, use magazine pictures that remind you of Halloween. Good ideas are leaves, creepy houses, pumpkins, and the moon.

Envelopes

You can make your own envelopes to fit your homemade cards.

THINGS YOU'LL NEED

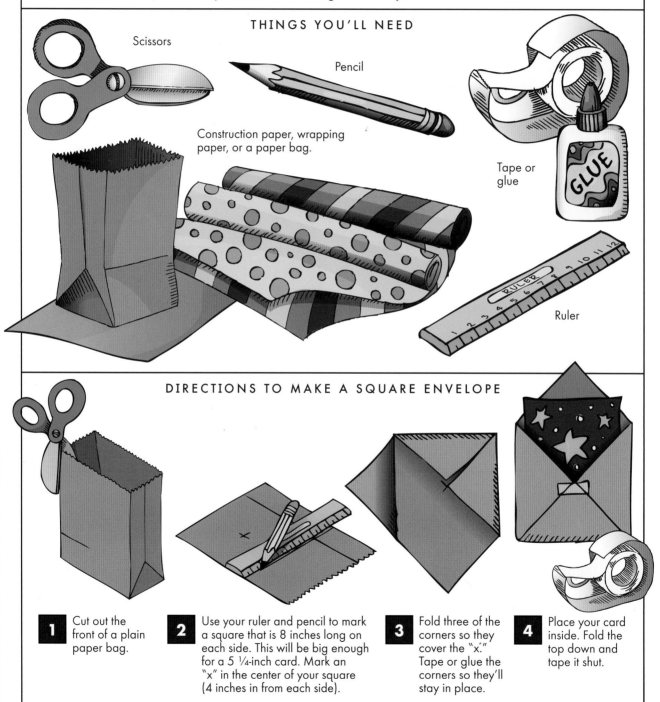

Scissors

Pencil

Construction paper, wrapping paper, or a paper bag.

Tape or glue

GLUE

RULER

Ruler

DIRECTIONS TO MAKE A SQUARE ENVELOPE

1 Cut out the front of a plain paper bag.

2 Use your ruler and pencil to mark a square that is 8 inches long on each side. This will be big enough for a 5 ¼-inch card. Mark an "x" in the center of your square (4 inches in from each side).

3 Fold three of the corners so they cover the "x." Tape or glue the corners so they'll stay in place.

4 Place your card inside. Fold the top down and tape it shut.

DIRECTIONS TO MAKE AN ENVELOPE THAT'S NOT SQUARE

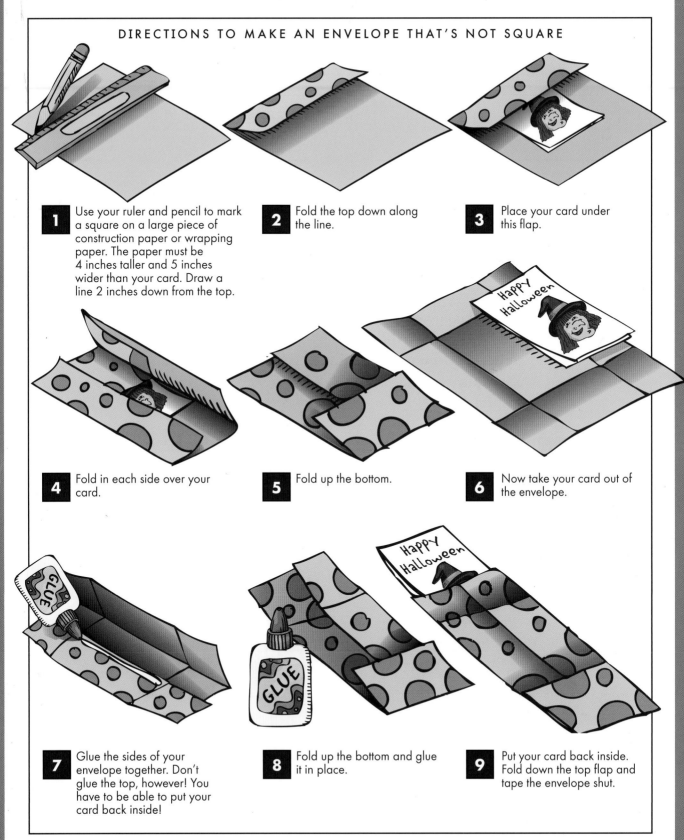

1 Use your ruler and pencil to mark a square on a large piece of construction paper or wrapping paper. The paper must be 4 inches taller and 5 inches wider than your card. Draw a line 2 inches down from the top.

2 Fold the top down along the line.

3 Place your card under this flap.

4 Fold in each side over your card.

5 Fold up the bottom.

6 Now take your card out of the envelope.

7 Glue the sides of your envelope together. Don't glue the top, however! You have to be able to put your card back inside!

8 Fold up the bottom and glue it in place.

9 Put your card back inside. Fold down the top flap and tape the envelope shut.

Activities

Halloween is a great time to invite your friends over for some fun activities. Here are some great ideas.

1 Take turns with your friends making silly or scary faces with face paints. You can also draw smaller things such as bats, pumpkins, and ghosts on your cheeks.

2 Hold a Halloween party! Decorate the room with the decorations from this book. You can add some orange and black **streamers**, too. Invite your friends over to play games and have fun. Make sure everyone wears a costume!

3 Have a Halloween parade during the day. Tell your friends to come over in their **costumes**. Then put on a parade in your neighborhood.

4 Hold a scarecrow party. Have people bring old clothes for making the scarecrow. Then stuff it with straw and leaves. Be sure to put it out for people to see on Halloween night!

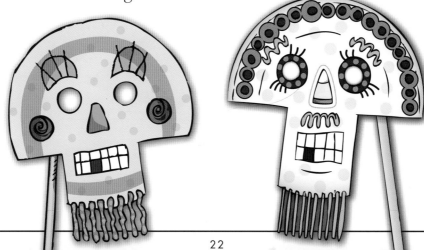

Glossary

acrylic (uh-KRIL-ik) Acrylic paints are thick and dry quickly. They are good to use in art projects.

costumes (KOS-toomz) Costumes are outfits people wear to look like someone or something else.

cultures (KUL-churz) Cultures are people's ways of life and traditions. Many cultures have celebrations to honor the dead.

directions (dir-EK-shunz) Directions are the steps for how to do something. You should follow the directions in this book to make your crafts.

holiday (HOL-uh-day) A holiday is a time for celebration, such as Christmas or Valentine's Day. Halloween is a holiday.

steamers (STREE-merz) Streamers are long strips of colorful paper or plastic. They are used as decorations.

Find More Crafts

BOOKS

Ross, Kathy and Sharon Lane Holm (illustrator). *All New Crafts For Halloween*. Brookfield, CT: The Millbrook Press, 2003.

Umnik, Sharon Dunn. *Easy-to-Do Holiday Crafts from Everyday Household Items!* Honesdale, PA: Boyds Mill Press, 1995.

WEB SITES

Visit our Web site for links to more crafts: childsworld.com/links

Note to Parents, Teachers, and Librarians: We routinely verify our Web links to make sure they are safe and active sites. So encourage your readers to check them out!

Index

ABOUT THE AUTHOR

Jean Eick has written over 200 books for children over the past forty years. She has written biographies, craft books, and many titles on nature and science. Jean lives in Lake Tahoe with her husband and enjoys hiking in the mountains, reading, and doing volunteer work.